The Digestive System

CHRISTINE TAYLOR-BUTLER

Children's Press®
An Imprint of Scholastic Inc.
New York Toronto London Auckland Sydney
Mexico City New Delhi Hong Kong
Danbury, Connecticut

Content Consultant
Lawrence J. Cheskin, M.D., F.A.C.P.
Associate Professor of Medicine
Johns Hopkins University School of Medicine
Baltimore, Maryland

Library of Congress Cataloging-in-Publication Data

Taylor-Butler, Christine.
 The Digestive system / by Christine Taylor-Butler.
      p. cm. -- (A true book)
 Includes bibliographical references and index.
     ISBN-13: 978-0-531-16857-8 (lib. bdg.)
              978-0-531-20731-4 (pbk.)
     ISBN-10: 0-531-16857-3 (lib. bdg.)
              0-531-20731-5 (pbk.)

1. Digestive organs--Juvenile literature. 2. Digestion--Juvenile
literature. I. Title. II. Series.

 QP145.T37 2008
 612.3--dc22   2007036013

Produced by Weldon Owen Education Inc.

1 2 3 4 5 6 7 8 9 10 R 17 16 15 14 13 12 11 10 09 08

Find the Truth!

Everything you are about to read is true *except* for one of the sentences on this page.

Which one is **TRUE**?

T or F Your small intestine is about five feet (1.5 meters) long.

T or F An acid strong enough to dissolve metal helps digest food in the stomach.

Find the answers in this book.

Contents

THE **BIG** TRUTH!

Food's Long Journey

People are not the only living things to eat cheese. The mold growing on blue cheese is enjoying it too!

Ice-cold drinks slow down the digestion process. Warm or room-temperature drinks are better for digestion.

CHAPTER 1

It's a Gas!

Burrrp! If you eat or drink too fast, you'll swallow too much air. This can cause you to belch.

You're having lunch with your grandparents. You're on your best behavior. But as you sip your soda, your stomach starts to feel strange. It feels very full. It aches. Then the worst possible thing happens. You belch loudly! Embarrassed? Probably, but don't feel too bad. It's your digestive system in action, and it's normal. Everyone belches.

When you eat and drink, you swallow gas as well as food. It could be air. It could be carbon dioxide from a fizzy drink. Sometimes the gas comes back out as a burp, or a belch.

Your stomach doesn't need gas, so it gets rid of it. What it needs is food. Food is the fuel that provides you with energy. Your body needs energy for moving, breathing, and even thinking.

Drinking bubbly drinks through a straw is a recipe for belching. You take in air through the straw as well as carbon dioxide from the drink.

Your digestive system slows down at night. However, it keeps breaking down food even when you are sleeping.

Your digestive system breaks food into small units that can be used by your body. Whatever you can't use is passed out of your body as waste.

Bacteria in your system change part of the waste into gas. Some of this gas is absorbed into your body. But other gases are released out of your digestive system through your **rectum**.

It may seem embarrassing. However, all people have gas in their digestive tract.

It is perfectly normal to pass gas as many as 20 times a day.

➡️

Food to Gas

Some foods cause people to have more gas than other foods do. Beans, for instance, are not completely digested by your small intestine. When the beans reach your large intestine, bacteria begin to feed on them. The bacteria produce large amounts of gas in the process. Most gas passes quietly. But sometimes it builds up pressure. It comes out at high speed. This creates that familiar sound.

Foods such as eggs and meat contain a lot of sulfur. When the bacteria in your stomach feed on these foods, they produce gases that smell like rotten eggs. Phew!

The digestive tract is
like a long, winding
tube. It is helped
by other organs
in the body,
such as the liver.

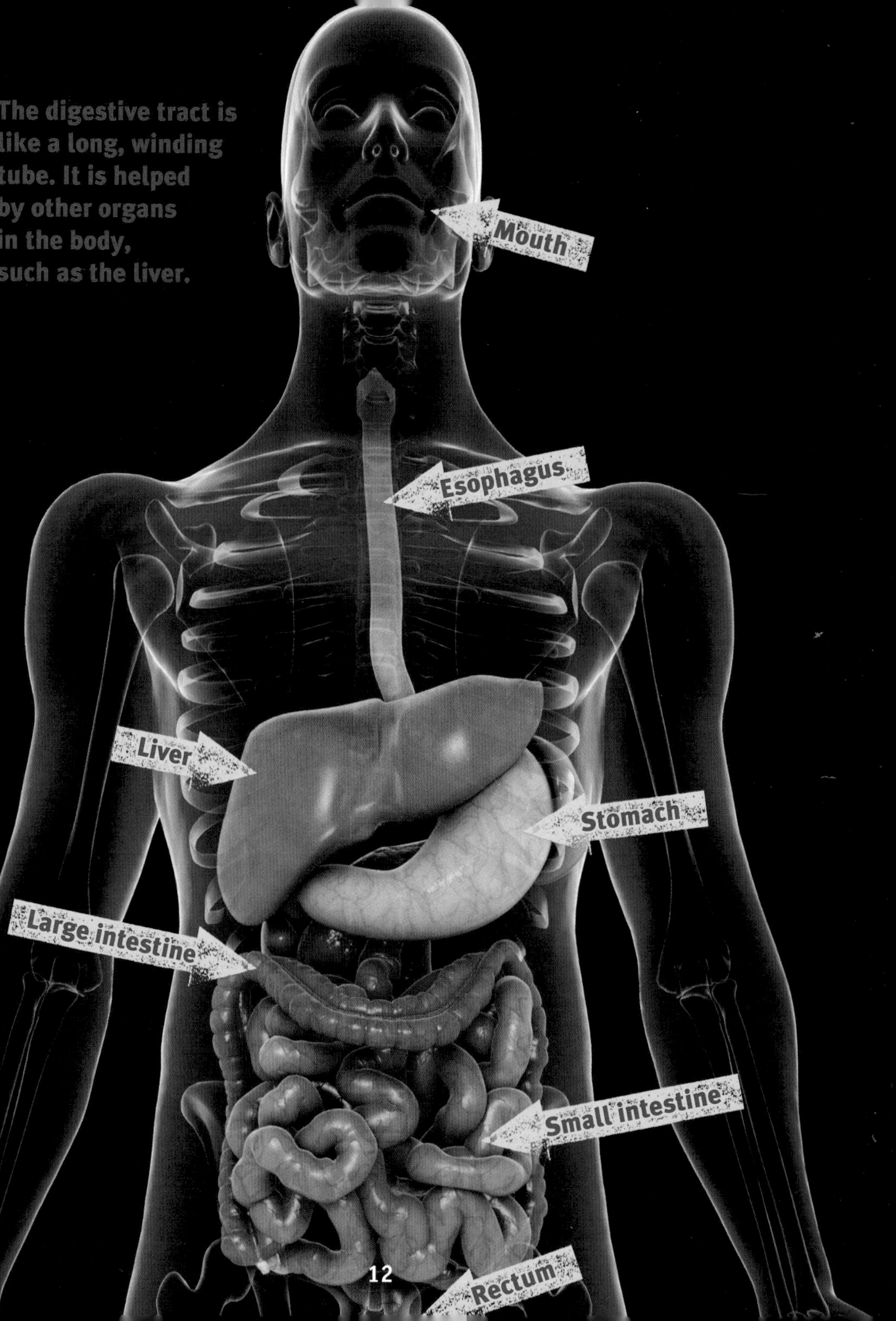

Mouth

Esophagus

Liver

Stomach

Large intestine

Small intestine

Rectum

CHAPTER 2

Your Food Processor

From one end to the other, the digestive tract is about 30 feet (9 meters) long.

Your digestive system has an important job. It breaks down food into tiny pieces. The nutrients, vitamins, and minerals in food can then pass into your bloodstream to be used by your body. Your digestive tract consists of six main parts: the mouth, **esophagus**, stomach, small intestine, large intestine, and rectum. Each part has its own task.

Chew on This!

Your body begins to break down, or digest, food as soon as it enters your mouth. Teeth break up the food into smaller pieces. Saliva is the liquid in your mouth. It is produced by salivary glands. It contains chemicals called enzymes (EN-zimes). These start to break down **starches** in your food even before it's swallowed. Saliva also contains a lot of water, which mixes with the food. This helps the food slide down your esophagus

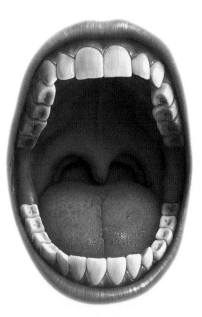

smoothly. Muscles around your esophagus squeeze, or contract, in waves. This action pushes food down the esophagus to your stomach.

Your front teeth cut and slice food. Your back teeth mash food.

Your body makes more
than one quart (0.95 liter)
of saliva each day. Mashed
food inside your esophagus
is called a bolus.

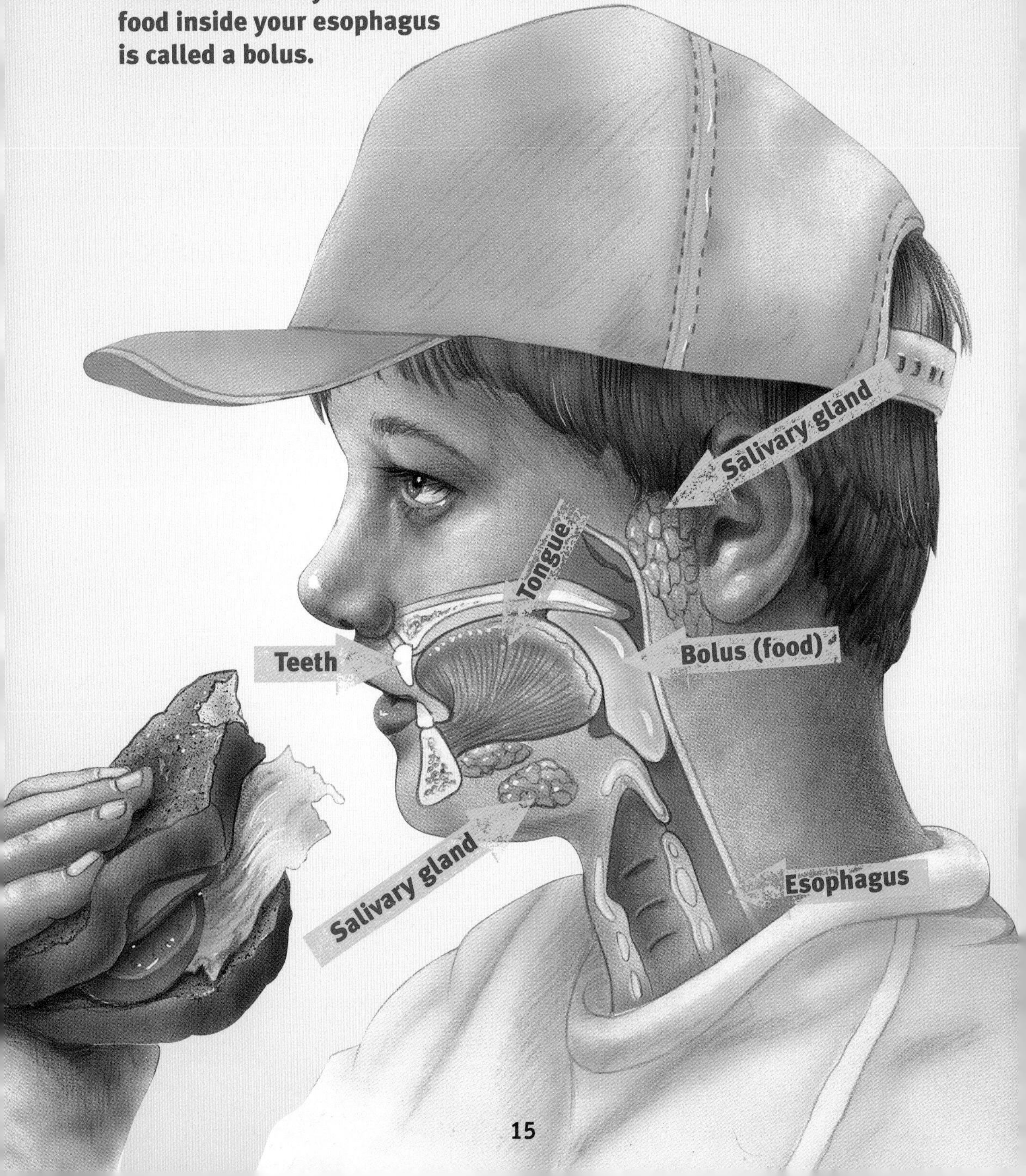

Salivary gland

Tongue

Teeth

Bolus (food)

Salivary gland

Esophagus

15

Don't Drink This Juice

Your stomach is made of strong muscles. It can stretch to hold about three pints (1.4 liters) of food at one time. When food enters your stomach, the muscles squeeze and mash your food into smaller and smaller pieces.

The cells lining your stomach release a liquid called **gastric** juice. It contains enzymes and hydrochloric acid. This acid is strong enough to dissolve metal. A **mucus** lining protects your stomach from the acid.

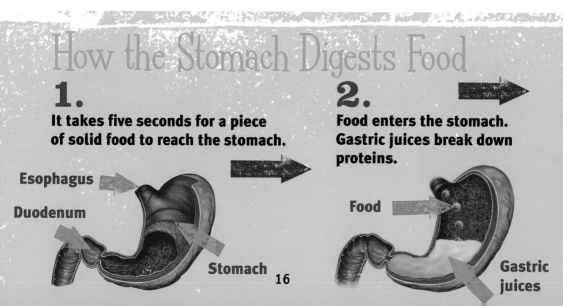

How the Stomach Digests Food

1.
It takes five seconds for a piece of solid food to reach the stomach.

2.
Food enters the stomach. Gastric juices break down proteins.

Esophagus

Duodenum

Stomach

Food

Gastric juices

Gastric juice begins to breaks down proteins. Proteins are found in foods such as meat, cheese, and eggs. Food stays in your stomach for two to five hours. Once it mixes with gastric juice, it is called chyme (kime). The stomach releases chyme into the duodenum (doo-uh-DEE-nuhm). This is the first part of the small intestine. A muscle called a sphincter relaxes to let a little chyme pass through. The sphincter then squeezes tightly to keep the rest in your stomach.

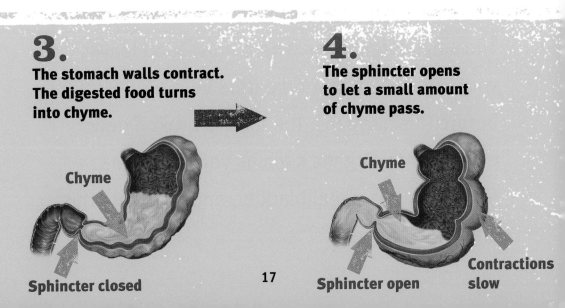

3.
The stomach walls contract. The digested food turns into chyme.

Chyme

Sphincter closed

4.
The sphincter opens to let a small amount of chyme pass.

Chyme

Sphincter open

Contractions slow

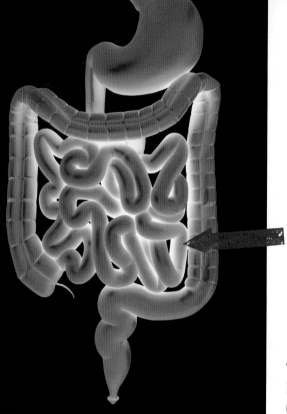

If you stretched out your small intestine, it would be almost 20 feet (6 meters) long!

The small intestine is about 1 to 2 inches (2.5 to 5 centimeters) wide.

It's Small, but It's Long

The small intestine is where most food leaves your digestive tract and enters your bloodstream. Before this happens, the food is broken down even further. Organs such as your pancreas (PAN-kree-uhss), gallbladder, and liver help this digestion happen.

Your pancreas squirts fluid into the duodenum. This fluid is rich in enzymes that break down fats, proteins, and starches. The fluid also contains a chemical that makes chyme less acidic. It is called sodium bicarbonate (SOH-dee-uhm bi-CAR-bin-ate).

Your gallbladder adds a liquid called bile to the chyme. Bile helps break up blobs of fat so that enzymes can get to it more easily. Bile is made in the liver. It is stored in the gallbladder.

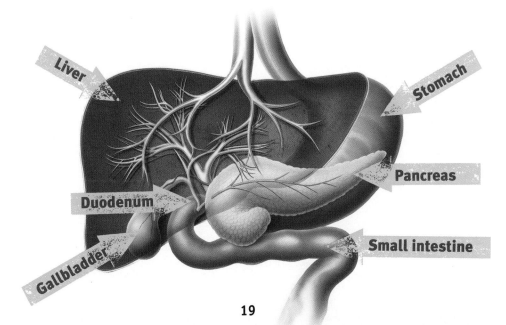

The small intestine has many folds. It is lined with millions of finger-shaped bumps called villi. This creates a huge surface area that can absorb large volumes of food quickly. Tiny blood vessels inside the villi absorb the nutrients straight into your bloodstream.

Each villus is covered with even smaller finger-shaped bumps. They are called microvilli.

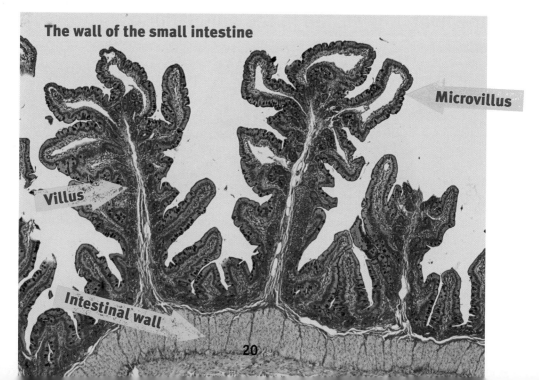

The wall of the small intestine

Microvillus

Villus

Intestinal wall

Nutrient-rich blood goes from your small intestine to your liver. The liver converts the nutrients into substances needed by the body. It stores some nutrients. It releases them into the blood when they are needed. The liver also breaks down harmful substances, such as alcohol.

If a surgeon accidentally cut off a piece of the liver, it would grow back!

Eating fresh fruits and vegetables is good for your liver. They contain enzymes, vitamins, and fiber that help with digestion.

The End of the Line

By the time the food reaches the end of the small intestine, most of the nutrients have been absorbed. The parts that your body can't use pass into your large intestine. This intestine is only five feet (1.5 meters) long. However, it is about three to four inches (7 to 10 centimeters) wide.

The large intestine is also called the colon. It absorbs minerals and water from indigestible food. This makes the waste more solid. Lumps of solid waste are called **feces**. Muscles push the feces along the colon to the rectum. They remain there until you go to the bathroom.

Kiwifruit contain a high amount of fiber. They help keep your large intestine healthy.

Digestive Tips

1. Eat at regular meal times.

2. Chew your food well.

3. Stop eating before you feel really full. The brain signals the feeling of fullness about ten minutes after you're actually full.

4. Relax! If you are relaxed, your body will produce more gastric juice.

5. Sit up straight when you eat so that your digestive tract is not cramped.

6. Avoid drinking lots of liquids half an hour before or after your meals.

7. Don't eat late at night. It takes your body longer to digest food when you are asleep.

12:02 P.M.

Your stomach begins to mash the bolus into chyme. Enzymes break down the proteins. Strong acid kills bacteria in the chyme. Chyme stays in the stomach for a few hours.

6:00 P.M.

The last part of the chyme that can't be digested enters your colon (large intestine). The colon absorbs water and minerals and transfers them back into the body.

6:00 A.M.

The waste enters your rectum. It waits there until you go to the bathroom.

3:00 P.M.

A squirt of chyme enters your duodenum. Your pancreas and gallbladder release liquids to help digest it. Villi in the small intestine transfer nutrients to your bloodstream.

Midnight

The undigested chyme is still traveling through your colon.

7:30 A.M.

The wastes come out as feces and are flushed away.

Rectum

Small intestine

Gallbladder

Liver

Esophagus

Bolus

Pancreas

Stomach

Colon

Food's Long Journey

It's lunchtime! You take the first bite of your sandwich and start chewing. You wash down that mouthful with some milk. However, swallowing is just the beginning of the journey. It may take 20 to 30 hours for this food to digest completely and for the waste to leave your body.

Noon

You take a bite of your sandwich. You chew it until it is mushy. Saliva helps break down the starches in the bread.

12:01 P.M.

The bolus of sandwich slides down your esophagus.

Your body can't digest food and move fast at the same time. This is why you feel sick if you exercise soon after a meal.

CHAPTER 3

Digestive Disorders

Have you ever had a stomachache? It tells you that your digestive system has a problem. Other signs that something is wrong include vomiting and **diarrhea**. They could be a sign that you have eaten the wrong foods or caught an infection. They can also indicate that you are under stress.

Got butterflies? When you're nervous, your stomach shuts down. This allows blood to go to other muscles. It causes a fluttery feeling.

Why Does My Stomach Hurt?

A stomachache could be caused by something you ate. Some people are allergic to foods such as wheat or nuts. Other people are lactose intolerant. They cannot digest dairy foods properly. Stomachaches can also be caused by eating a poisonous food, such as some types of mushroom.

Lactose intolerance affects as much as 75 percent of the world's population.

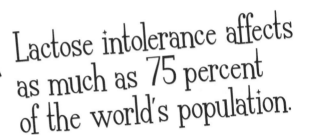

In the small intestine, an enzyme called lactase breaks down lactose. Lactose is a sugar in milk. People who are lactose intolerant do not have enough lactase to break down the lactose in large quantities of dairy foods.

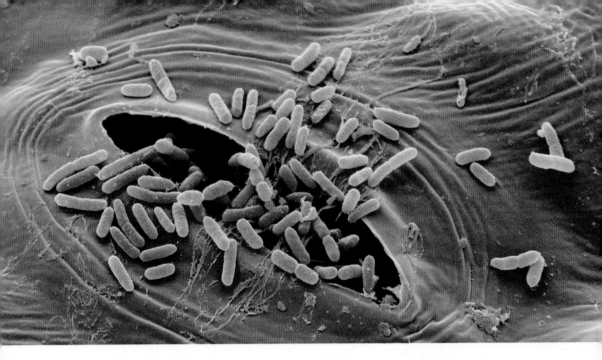

The purple shapes in this microscope image are bacteria. They are on a lettuce leaf.

Food can contain **microbes**, such as bacteria. Fortunately, most microbes are killed before they can harm you. Some, however, cause food poisoning. Many produce toxins that poison your body. The symptoms include cramps, vomiting, and diarrhea. It may take several days before your body gets all the germs out of your digestive tract. You may need to see a doctor.

Throwing Up

You have probably had to throw up at some stage in your life. Vomiting is certainly unpleasant. However, it has a useful purpose. It is often your body's way of getting rid of poisons before they get into your bloodstream. The muscles in your abdomen squeeze your stomach. This forces the stomach to empty its contents back up the esophagus and out through your mouth.

Vomiting is a reflex. Once it starts, there's nothing you can do to stop it.

Heartburn and Ulcers

Usually a ring of muscle keeps food in the stomach from going back up your esophagus. Sometimes a problem keeps it from closing properly. Stomach acid may then get into your esophagus. This causes a burning feeling called heartburn.

Some stomachaches are caused by ulcers. Ulcers are wounds in the stomach lining. They allow gastric juice to attack the stomach wall. Ulcers are often caused by a particular bacterium. Doctors use an **antibiotic** to kill the bacteria. They use **antacids** to reduce the acid in the gastric juice while the wounds heal.

Eating smaller meals and avoiding spicy or fatty foods can help prevent heartburn. Antacids can take away the pain.

Colon Care

Sometimes what you call a stomachache is actually pain in your large intestine. If you haven't drunk enough water or eaten the right foods, you may be **constipated**. If you have an infection in your large intestine, your body will want to get rid of it fast. The result is diarrhea.

Sometimes the same symptoms indicate a more serious disease, such as colon cancer. In these cases, a surgeon may remove the unhealthy section of the colon and reconnect the two ends.

It's important to drink water when you are thirsty.

What's It For?

Your appendix (uh-PEN-diks) is a small tube at the start of your large intestine. Scientists are not sure why it is there. Some think it might help fight infections. However, people who have had their appendix removed have no obvious problems.

Sometimes the appendix becomes swollen and inflamed. This condition is called appendicitis. It can cause a sharp pain in the side, fever, and vomiting. People who think they have appendicitis must see a doctor right away. If the appendix is not removed in time, it will burst. This can cause a serious infection that is sometimes fatal.

Large intestine

Appendix

CHAPTER 4

Call the Experts

It can be hard to figure out what's causing a digestive problem. Your body will fix problems such as gas or a mild infection on its own. More serious problems require advice from a doctor.

If your doctor is unsure what is wrong, he or she might send you to a gastroenterologist (gas-troh-en-tuh-ROL-uh-jist). That's a doctor who is an expert on the digestive system.

In the word *gastroenterologist*, *gastro* means "stomach" and *entero* means "intestine."

The First Stomach Surgeon

Years ago, doctors didn't understand the digestive system. They had no way of seeing inside the body. This started to change in 1822. A fur trapper named Alexis St. Martin accidentally shot himself in the stomach. The wound healed, but a fist-sized hole through his skin and into his stomach remained.

Surgeon William Beaumont used the hole to study the digestive system. He would tie string to a piece of food and push the food into the hole. He then pulled it out at various times to figure out the steps in the digestion process. Beaumont also discovered that the stomach acid broke down food on its own.

When St. Martin died, his family let the body rot for four days before burying it. They wanted to make sure that no one could do any more experiments on him.

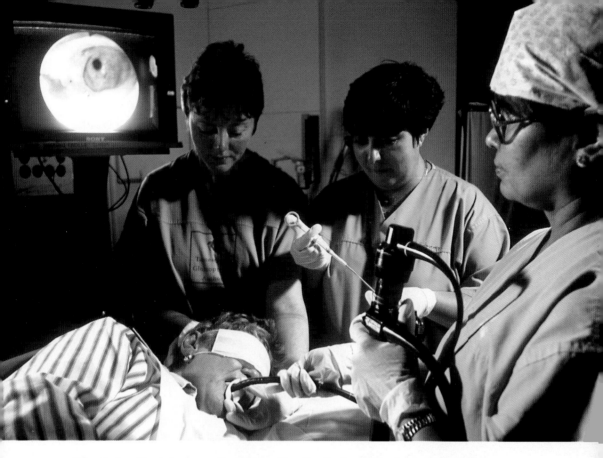

The tube that is inserted into the body is called an endoscope.

Today, doctors can look inside your digestive tract without cutting you open. They insert a special tube with a light and a camera at the end into your body. The end of the tube also has a tiny device that can take a sample of your tissue so that the doctor can study it in a lab.

If you eat regular, healthful meals, you will get all the vitamins and minerals you need.

CHAPTER 5

Fit for Life

If a meal is late, your stomach might growl. It's contracting, and releasing juices ready for your food.

How do you keep your digestive tract in top shape? Eat well, drink water when you are thirsty, and get regular exercise. If you do these things, the good things will get into your system and the unwanted waste will move out quickly. You'll feel well. You'll have all the energy you need.

Put in Only the Best

Fiber helps keep your intestines healthy. Fiber is the material in plant cells that helps them hold their shape. Fruits, vegetables, and whole grains, such as cereals and breads, are full of fiber. Your body doesn't absorb fiber. Instead, it uses the fiber to help push material through the intestines quickly.

Water is also important for keeping things moving in your intestines. It can help you avoid hard feces, which lead to constipation. Water also helps the body absorb vitamins and minerals.

Too much fat in your food can slow your digestion.

Digestion Times

It takes different amounts of time for the stomach to digest different types of foods. Eating food in the order of its digestion can help the digestive process. That way, the slowly digested foods will not hold up the other foods.

20-30 minutes

★ Water
★ Juices

30-45 minutes

★ Fruits
★ Vegetables
★ Soups

2-3 hours

★ Beans
★ Grains
★ Nuts

2-5 hours

★ Milk
★ Cheeses

3 or more hours

★ Many meats

Keep on Track!

Exercise is important for keeping your digestive tract on track. Moving your body helps food move through your intestines. Don't do vigorous exercise right after eating though. Wait a half hour after a snack, or up to three hours after a heavy meal.

If you look after your digestive tract, it will look after you. Put healthful food in, and your body will convert it into a healthy body and plenty of energy. ★

Vigorous exercise after a meal can cause muscle weakness. However, gentle walking can help digestion.

Average amount of food a person eats per year:
1,100 pounds (500 kilograms)
Amount of time it takes to chew a mouthful of food:
About 5 to 30 seconds
Length of an adult esophagus:
About 10 to 14 inches (25 to 35 centimeters)
**Average amount of hydrochloric acid produced
in a person's stomach each day:** About 4 pints
(1.7 liters)
Amount of time food usually stays in the colon:
18 hours to 2 days
Number of species of bacteria in a person's colon:
More than 400

Did you find the truth?

F Your small intestine is about
five feet (1.5 meters) long.

T An acid strong enough to dissolve
metal helps digest food in the stomach.

Resources

Books

Ballard, Carol. *The Stomach and Digestion*. New York: Franklin Watts, 2005.

DK Publishing. *Alive: The Living, Breathing Human Body Book*. New York: DK Children, 2007.

Jakab, Cheryl. *Digestive System*. Mankato, MN: Smart Apple Media, 2007.

Martineau, Susan and Hel James. *Healthy Eating*. Mankato, MN: Smart Apple Media, 2006.

Parker, Steve. *Break It Down: The Digestive System*. Chicago: Raintree, 2006.

Silverstein, Dr. Alvin and Virginia, and Laura Silverstein Nunn. *Eat Your Vegetables! Drink Your Milk!* (My Health). New York: Franklin Watts, 2000.

Simon, Seymour. *Guts: Our Digestive System*. New York: HarperCollins, 2005.

Taylor-Butler, Christine. *The Food Pyramid* (A True Book™: Health and the Human Body). New York: Children's Press, 2008.

Organizations and Web Sites

Hillendale Health
http://hes.ucf.k12.pa.us/gclaypo/digestive_system.html
Do the quizzes to test your knowledge of the digestive system.

Human Body Adventure
http://vilenski.org/science/humanbody/hb_html/
digestivesystem.html
Take a close look at the organs involved in the digestive system.

Yucky Discovery
http://yucky.discovery.com/noflash/body/pg000126.html
Scroll down "Pick a body function" to learn what makes your stomach gurgle and why you belch.

Place to Visit

Adventure Science Center
800 Fort Negley Blvd.
Nashville, TN 37203
615-862-5160
www.adventuresci.com/exhibits
Visit the interactive BodyQuest exhibit. See what goes on inside your body every day.

Important Words

antacid – a substance that makes an acid less strong

antibiotic (an-tie-bie-OT-ik) – a medicine that kills bacteria

bacteria – tiny, one-celled living things. Some bacteria cause disease.

constipated – unable to easily empty the bowels

diarrhea (die-uh-REE-uh) – a condition in which feces leave the body before much water has been removed

esophagus (i-SOF-uh-guhss) – the tube that connects your throat to your stomach

feces (FEE-seez) – the undigested food that is removed from your body as waste

gastric – to do with the stomach

microbe – a tiny living thing, such as a virus or bacteria, that is too small to see without a microscope

mucus (MYOO-kuhss) – a slimy fluid that protects the breathing passages and the stomach

rectum – the end of the large intestine

starch – a kind of food that provides the body with energy. It is sometimes called carbohydrate.

Index

About the Author

Christine Taylor-Butler lives in Kansas City, Missouri, with her husband and two daughters. A native of Ohio, she is the author of more than 40 books for children. She holds a B.S. degree in both Civil Engineering and Art and Design from the Massachusetts Institute of Technology in Cambridge, MA. Other books by Ms. Taylor-Butler in the True Book Health and the Human Body series include: *The Food Pyramid*, *Food Allergies*, *Food Safety*, *The Circulatory System*, *The Respiratory System*, and *The Nervous System*.

PHOTOGRAPHS© 2008: Big Stock Photo (back cover; p. 4; cheese, p. 5; p. 11; p. 28; pp. 31–33; vegetables, beans and nuts, p. 41); Getty Images (cover; organs, p. 5; p. 6; p. 12); Ingram Image Library (meats, p. 41); iStockPhoto.com (p. 8; ©Daniel Bendjy, p. 3; ©Branislav Senic, p. 21; ©Anette Romanenko, p. 23; ©Jim Kolaczko, p. 42); Photodisc (p. 11; p. 22); Photolibrary (p. 10; p. 18; p. 20; p. 26; pp. 29–30; pp. 36–37); Stock.XCHNG(p. 40; glass of juice, bowl of rice, p. 41); Tranz/Corbis (p. 9; p. 34; p. 38). All other images property of Weldon Owen Education.